Pet Birds

Pet Birds

by Joan Joseph

Illustrated by John Hamberger

FRANKLIN WATTS, INC. • NEW YORK

1975

Library of Congress Cataloging in Publication Data

Joseph, Joan.
    Pet birds.

    (A Concise guide)
    Bibliography: p.
    Includes index.
    SUMMARY: Discusses the different breeds of
birds available as pets and the care, food, and
housing they require.
    1. Cage-birds—Juvenile literature. [1. Birds.
2. Pets] I. Hamberger, John. II. Title.
SF461.J68   636.6′8   75–11902
ISBN 0–531–02837–2

Contents

Introduction

Birds, probably man's oldest pet, are thought to be the youngest animal in the chain of evolution. They are believed to have descended indirectly from reptiles—a concept which is plausible when comparing a reptile's skin with the scaly skin of a bird's legs.

Although some 8600 species of birds have been identified, choosing the right bird for a pet is not difficult and can be lots of fun. There are a few basic considerations that every prospective bird owner should keep in mind:

First, make certain that no one in your family is allergic to birds. This is not usually a problem, but if one member of your family is particularly sensitive to pillow feathering, it is advisable that an allergy test be taken.

The next point to consider is where you live. If your home is a small apartment, a mynah bird, which is very noisy, may disturb your neighbors; in these quarters, a large parrot may be overbearing. On the other hand, small birds can be housed anywhere. If you live in a house with a backyard, you may wish to build an aviary and tame wild birds; but be aware that American law prohibits the caging of most native birds, since ecologically they are an important factor in keeping weeds and insects under control. Crows, jays, and magpies, however, are not protected by law and can become wonderful pets. Crows in particular make interesting pets, as they can be taught to talk. Furthermore, caring for a crow is very easy; it is a hardy bird and will eat virtually any food it can swallow. Always keep in mind that you will have most success taming and training a crow—or any bird—if you obtain the bird as a fledgling. The only requirements necessary to teach a crow to speak are time and patience. Don't believe the story that before a crow can talk you must split its tongue. This is a foolish and quite false tale.

What about foreign birds? Most countries have laws governing the capture and exportation of their native birds; nevertheless, until recently many species of exotic birds were available in pet stores, and foreign birds were the pride and joy of numerous bird owners in the United States. In 1972, however, there was an outbreak of reniket, a virus carried by wild birds which attacked fowl such as chicken, ducks, and geese. In order to protect our domestic fowl from this disease, which is almost always fatal, the government passed a law forbidding the importation of birds into the United States. In choosing a bird, therefore, your choice is now limited to birds bred in this country, but don't despair; there still is a wide selection available.

Buying a Bird

The best place to buy a bird is from a reliable pet store. Birds can also be purchased from mail-order houses. Your local pet shop or your librarian can direct you to magazines such as *Cagebirds* that list mail-order houses. If you order your bird by mail, make certain that the bird shipped to you is under guarantee. In some areas of the country there are bird farms; here you will find a large variety of cage birds for sale.

Price

In choosing a bird, price may be a very important factor. The price of a bird is often determined by its age and sex. A bird that has been tamed and trained is more expensive than a baby bird. An exotic bird is, of course, more expensive than a domestic bird. Coloring can also affect the price tag placed on a bird. Remember, an inexpensive pet bird can be just as much fun as a costly one.

Health

It is important to choose a healthy bird. Once you have made your choice, examine the bird carefully:

- Its chest should be full and meaty.
- Be certain that the feathers around its anal pore are dry. A yellow wetness around this area means diarrhea. Diarrhea can be fatal.
- Check that the wings and tail feathers are fully developed.
- Inspect the bird's face. Be sure that the eyes are clear, that there is no crusty formation around the beak, and that the nostrils are dry.

A healthy bird is alert to its surroundings; it is constantly moving about in its cage and is interested in its food and water. If one bird in the cage is sick—BEWARE—make certain that the ailment is not contagious. A reliable pet dealer will tell you if the bird you have chosen is in good health.

Age

If you have the time and patience to tame and train your bird, you should buy as young a bird as possible.

Care

If you have wondered if some birds are easier to care for than others, the answer is that no bird can be neglected. A bird, like every animal, needs daily care, love, and attention. If you are not willing to take on this responsibility, then a bird is not for you. The special care of an individual bird can be found by looking up that specific bird in the Contents.

Outfitting
Your Bird

Cage

The cage you choose will, of course, depend upon the size of your bird and its habits. The height of your cage is important, but its width is also a major consideration; the wingspan of your bird must be taken into account. If you buy a cage which is too small for your bird to fly about, be certain that it is allowed to exercise by flying around the room.

If you decide to build your own cage, it is important that you use nontoxic paint which contains NO lead. If the paint is guaranteed to be safe for babies, you can be confident that it won't harm your bird.

Perching Stations

All birds need exercise and, once tamed, should be allowed to fly around the room for an hour or so daily. In addition to a cage, therefore, your bird should have a few perching stations with toys attached somewhere outside the cage. Perching stations and outside playpens are commercially available at reasonable prices.

A clever bird will quickly learn how to unfasten its cage door. So remember, once you start allowing your bird to fly about, you must be certain to fasten the latch of its cage when it returns home.

Water and Seed Cups

You will need a minimum of three cups. Water and seed cups are usually interchangeable. The best kind of cup to buy is one designed with a hood that will protect the contents of the cup from your bird's droppings. Some birds, such as canaries

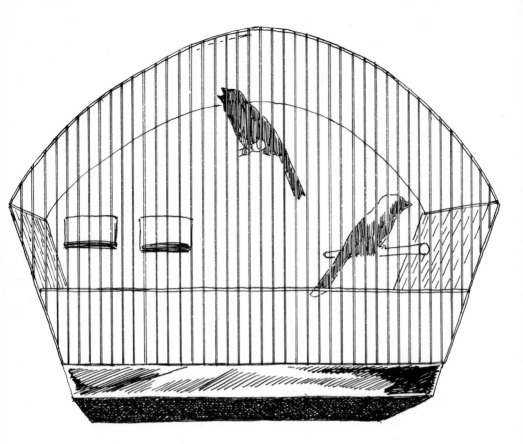

Choose a cage that will
suit your bird and its habits.

and finches, will drink and eat from cups attached to the outside of their cages; these cups are designed with an oblong piece that juts into the cage. Parrots and related birds, however, prefer inside cups.

Never place a water or seed cup on the bottom of the cage as your bird will undoubtedly overturn it.

Every bird needs fresh water daily. Water that has been boiled for at least fifteen minutes and cooled to room temperature is preferable to tap water. The drinking cup should be washed daily, as scum forms on the edges of the cup. This scum is a bacteria which may cause diarrhea and other serious ailments.

The seed cup should be cared for just like the water cup. Seed should be changed daily and the cup should be washed thoroughly and well dried. Proper care of seed cups will greatly reduce the probabilities of your bird becoming sick.

Health Grit

Most birds need grit to help them grind up the seed and other foods that they eat. It is advisable to keep grit in a separate cup. Suitable grit can easily be made by mixing four parts of crushed oyster shell with two parts bird gravel and one part bird charcoal. These items are obtained at your pet store and are very inexpensive; they are essential for your bird's health. The oyster shell will supply your bird with calcium; the gravel is imperative for digestion, and the charcoal will keep the food from souring during the digestive process. The food a bird eats remains in its gizzard until it is ground up and can proceed into the stomach.

Cuttlebone

A cuttlebone is an important item to have in the cage as it will supply your bird with minerals; these are a necessary part of your bird's diet. A cuttlebone will also help your bird keep its beak trimmed. It should be changed monthly.

Greens

All birds can be fed chopped spinach, lettuce, carrot tops, dandelion leaves, and clover, provided that they are fresh, clean, and damp. Be certain to wash your greens very well, as they are often sprayed with insecticides that are poisonous to birds.

Growing Greens

Fill an eight-inch to ten-inch flowerpot saucer with rich, moist soil. Plant bird seeds in the soil and keep the soil moist, *not* wet. The seeds will sprout within a few days. When the greenery reaches two to three inches in height, place the saucer in the cage and give your pet a healthy treat. You should have seven or eight saucers planted at all times so that you never run out of fresh greens.

Birdbath

A birdbath is usually a plastic, oval dish—large enough for your pet to hop about in and small enough to be placed at the bottom of the cage. Some baths are also hooded. These can be hung on the outside of the cage so that the hood surrounds the door and the bird can enter and leave without being able to fly out of the cage. Never fill the bath more than halfway; the water should be lukewarm. Leave the bath in place long enough to allow your pet to finish bathing.

Because a bird may decide to drink its bath water, it is advisable to treat the bath water and birdbath dish just as you do the drinking water and cup.

Gravel

The bottom of a well-made cage is equipped with a removable tray for easy cleaning. It is advisable to line this tray with newspaper before sprinkling it with gravel. Special fitted sheets of paper are available at pet stores, but these are an added, unnecessary expense. Sandpaper sheets, which are also available, should be avoided, as the friction of the paper on

*Birds need a
cuttlebone in their cage.*

the bird's feet can cause sores which may become infected and even be fatal.

Perches
All cages should be equipped with several perches. Wooden or plastic perches are fine. Sandpaper perches should be avoided.

Toys
Toys can be fun for a bird, but be careful not to clutter your cage. Canaries and finches love to swing, whereas budgerigars prefer climbing up and down a ladder. A mirror is almost a necessity for parrots, budgies, and other talking birds who can be amused for hours just looking at themselves. These birds also often enjoy playing with a tiny hanging bell.

Cage Cover
Many people like to cover their bird's cage at night. If your bird is in a draft-free location, the night air will not be harmful. Using a cover, therefore, is a choice you are free to make; it will not affect your bird one way or the other.

Caring for Your Bird

Once you have brought your bird home you must decide where to put the cage. The most important things to remember are:

Drafts
Keep your bird out of drafts. One cold draft is sufficient to give your bird pneumonia which is usually fatal.

Sunlight
Birds like sunlight, but both the direct rays of the sun and its glare are harmful. If your bird is exposed to the sun for an extended period of time, it will probably die.

Temperature
Most birds bought from a pet shop are bred to be kept indoors. They cannot tolerate extremes of heat and cold.

Hazards
Beware of your pet flying into fans, fires, fireplaces, and other devices for cooling or heating a room.

Other Pets
You can either place your cage on a table or suspend it from a ceiling, but be careful that it is out of the reach of other pets in the family.

Cleaning the Cage
Keeping the cage clean is of utmost importance. A dirty cage will soon develop a putrid smell. The cage can be cleaned within a few minutes if it is tended to daily. The floor should be

cleaned at least three times a week. The cage should be thoroughly washed once a month by scalding it with boiling water and spraying it with a good bird disinfectant solution. Once the cage is thoroughly dry, it should be dusted with a mite-killing powder. Be sure to put powder into the crevices of the cage and under the removable tray. Mite powder should also be dusted into and under the feathers of your bird approximately every six weeks. Mites are a problem in that they usually enter the house with birdseed and multiply rapidly if care is not taken.

Perches

Never clean the perches of your cage with water. Wooden perches will absorb the water, dry, and eventually splinter. Furthermore, perches that swell with water may give your bird rheumatism. The best method of cleaning perches is to scrape them with the edge of a sharp knife or with a special perch brush.

Trimming Your Bird's Nails

The nails or claws of your bird should be clipped two to three times a year. All you need is a pair of regular nail clippers, but be careful not to cut your pet. A bird has a vein in each claw. You must clip the claw above this vein. If you cut the vein, you will hurt your bird and its foot will bleed; this can be a very serious injury. The vein is easily visible, however, so you should not have any trouble. If you don't feel at ease about clipping your bird's claws, take your pet to a veterinarian or to your pet dealer.

Taming
Your Bird

When you first bring your new pet home, remember that it may be scared. Start by talking softly to it or even whistling a tune; many birds enjoy listening to music on the radio. Once you feel that your bird really feels at home, you can begin to tame it. Start by placing your hand on the outside of the cage. As soon as your bird remains calm at the sight of your hand, you can try putting your hand inside the cage. If the bird becomes frightened and begins to flap its wings in panic, remain still. Jerking your hand will frighten your bird even more.

Within a few days your bird will begin to accept your hand and may even come and perch on your finger. Now place some seeds in the palm of your hand. Once again it may take a few days, or even a week, but eventually your bird should eat out of your hand. Occasionally it may be necessary to remove the seed cup to convince your little pet that it should eat from your hand, but don't forget to return the cup within two or three hours. A small bird eats small amounts all day long. A feed cup that is missing for a prolonged period of time can cause starvation and death.

Once you have taught your pet to perch on your hand, you are ready to teach it to sit on your finger. Put your hand into the cage, extend your index finger, and, very, very gently, place it on the bird's breast, pressing just firmly enough so that it has to leave its perch and either step onto your finger or fly to another perch. Once you see that your bird is contentedly sitting on your finger, you can begin to move your hand around the cage.

After several weeks you will find that each time you put your hand into the cage your bird flies to you and perches on

your finger without any coaxing. It is at this time that your bird is ready to be let out of its cage.

The first time you let your bird free can be a most frightening experience for both you and your pet:

- Be sure that all windows and doors are closed.
- Be certain no one in the room is afraid of a bird when it is flying.
- Allow plenty of time for your bird to fly around. It will come back to you or fly directly to its cage as soon as it is tired.
- Mirrors can be dangerous, as can clear glass, curtainless, and blind-free windows. An unsuspecting bird may fly headlong into glass and have a fatal concussion.

So beware—look around the room carefully before allowing your pet its new freedom.

Teaching your
new pet to sit
on your finger

Training Your Bird

The younger a bird, the easier it will be to train. In addition, a single bird in a cage can be trained more easily than a bird with companions.

Some trainers find that clipping the feathers of one wing makes the task of training a bird easier. This can be true, since a bird that cannot fly will usually pay more attention to its trainer. Other trainers, however, find that wing clipping makes a bird so insecure that training becomes even more difficult.

Before making a decision, keep in mind that a bird's flight is its only means of protection. A bird hopping around on the floor can easily be stepped on or fall prey to a pet cat. Also, a bird with a clipped wing is not able to exercise as much as it should.

If you do decide upon clipping, clip only one wing. Clip the outer primaries on the front of the wing at the outer ends. Do not clip away the whole quill. Each quill is hollow at the ends; if you clip the primary at its base, the bird will bleed profusely and have a great deal of pain. Clipping the outer feathers, however, is painless. If while clipping your bird you are afraid that it may nip your hand, wrap a large towel around it, exposing only the wing to be clipped.

Once you have tamed your bird so that it is not afraid of perching on your finger inside the cage, you should have no difficulty training it to perch on your finger outside its cage. When it is finger-trained, try teaching it to jump from the floor to your finger. Keep repeating the words "hop" and "sit" until it hops onto your finger and sits quietly. Each time your bird succeeds in following your command, praise it. You can also

Clipping your pet's wing

offer it a few seeds. Food is an excellent reward and is of great help in training.

Teaching Birds to Talk

Teaching a bird to talk can be lots of fun, but it does require patience, and you will naturally have to choose one of the talking birds (see Contents page). Birds, like babies, don't learn to talk in one day. It can take as long as a year, and sometimes even longer, to teach your pet to mimic words.

It is almost impossible to teach a bird to talk if there is another bird in the cage. The key to teaching your bird is to position the cage so that nothing distracts it. Some trainers suggest covering three sides and the top of the cage so that your bird can see only you.

Begin your lessons with one or two simple words such as: "Hi, Bobbie" or "Pretty Birdie." Repeat these words over and over. Every time you walk near the cage repeat the words. Do not say anything else to your bird except the words you are trying to teach it to say. Try to use the same inflection in your voice each time you repeat the words. Then one day, weeks or even months later, your bird will surprise you and softly repeat your words. Once you have taught your bird its first words, you should have no difficulty teaching it many phrases. You can teach it specific questions and responses and even bits of poetry. Remember, these little creatures have no reasoning power. Don't ask your bird a question and expect an answer. A bird cannot think up a sentence; it can only repeat what it has been taught.

One of the easiest ways to teach your bird to talk is to buy a record or tape with just one phrase repeated over and over again. Your local pet dealer should be able to obtain these records for you.

Teaching Birds to Sing

Teaching a bird to sing is similar to teaching it to talk. It takes time and patience. Canaries, for example, are famous for their song, but they often need a little help before they begin singing. The best way to teach a bird to sing is to purchase a record of a well-trained singing bird. When playing the record, place your bird near the record player in a position in the room that is free from distraction. Some people find that darkening the surroundings helps a bird to concentrate on the music and, consequently, learn to sing more quickly.

The best way to be certain that your bird will entertain

you with its singing is to purchase one that already sings. Your pet dealer should be willing to give you a written guarantee that you are buying a singer. If your bird doesn't sing within three weeks of bringing it home, exchange it for another bird. However, a bird has to be taken care of to be happy; your bird has to want to sing.

Talking Birds

BUDGERIGARS
Popular name: budgie or parrakeet

Although there are innumerable genera of parrakeets, the Australian Budgerigar or Grass Parrakeet is perhaps the most popular cage bird in the world. In America alone, there are more than twelve million pet budgerigars.

The budgerigar is commonly known in the United States as a parrakeet, whereas in Britain it is called a budgie. The popular term parrakeet, however, is not its scientific name, as the budgerigar is the only member of its genus and cannot be grouped with exotic birds such as the Crested Parrakeet, native to the South Pacific, or the White Winged Parrakeet from the Amazon Valley. To differentiate, therefore, between the many genera of parrakeets and the budgerigar, the term budgie will be used throughout this book.

The Australian aborigines, the Bushmen, must be credited with having named the first wild budgie. They called the light green bird with its lemon-yellow face and throat "betcherry-gah" or "budgerigar," which translated means "pretty bird" or "good bird."

Budgies were not known in the Western world until about 1840, when the famous ornithologist John Gould brought the first budgies from Australia to England. Before long it was discovered that budgies made excellent pets. They were hardy in captivity; they had a long life span, were easily cared for, could be taught to speak, and were able to acquire a fairly large vocabulary.

Budgerigars are among
the most charming of pets.

Sailors, learning how easy it was to care for and train a budgie, soon preferred sailing with these small companions instead of their larger cousins, the parrot. These "pretty birds" became so popular in Europe that by 1884 the Australian government, fearing that the budgie might become extinct, banned the exportation of the birds except for scientific study. Aviculturists, however, had already discovered that budgerigars breed easily and multiply very rapidly. For example, a single pair of budgies can produce as many as forty eggs in one year. Aviculturists also found that budgies could be bred for color. After careful study, they succeeded in breeding budgies in a large variety of colors. Today budgies range from snow white and bright yellow to cobalt blue and pinkish mauve; the rarest color produced to date is an intense shade of violet. At present breeders are experimenting with colors in the hope that they will succeed in breeding a bright red budgie.

Description of a Budgie

Since the age of a budgie will often determine how successful you will be in training your little pet, it is important to know how to tell a bird's age. There are two points to remember:

1. Look at the bird's forehead. Baby birds have striped black feathers on their foreheads. As the bird matures, these stripes will fade and eventually disappear. Be careful; don't confuse the black striped feathers on the back and the head of a bird with those on the forehead. These former striped areas never fade, although on yellow and white budgies they are less distinct.

2. Look at the bird's cere. The cere is a waxy piece of skin that grows just above the bird's beak. In birds under four months old, the cere is usually a light blue or a light violet color. In older birds the cere darkens considerably. The adult male's cere will deepen to a dark blue, whereas the adult female's will change to a light tan or brown, especially during mating season.

Type of Cage

Although budgies can survive in a small cage—nine inches by twelve inches—they love to climb, roll, and tumble and will be happier in a cage large enough for them to practice their acrobatic antics. Make certain that the cage is made out of unpainted metal. Budgies love to chew at a wooden cage and will soon escape. Likewise, perches should be made of hard wood so that your pet cannot chew and splinter the perch. Toys also should be made of plastic, metal, or hardwood.

Feeding Your Budgie

A budgie needs fresh food and water daily. The food is easily available at your local pet shop. You may either buy packaged Parrakeet Seed Mixture or your pet dealer may mix his own seed. To ensure that your bird has a balanced diet, be certain that the mixture contains canary seed, whole hulled oats, and large millet seed.

Once or twice a week you can give your pet some green food. Don't leave greens in the cage for more than forty-five minutes. A bird that overeats its greens will get diarrhea. Leave greens damp, as budgies love to roll in the wet, grasslike vegetables, and this may be considered an occasional substitute for a bath.

HEALTH GRIT should be changed regularly, about three times a week.

WATER must be changed daily and should be cool but *not* cold.

CUTTLEBONE should be changed once a month.

WHEAT GERM OIL is an excellent aid in keeping your bird healthy. Add a few drops on top of your bird's food three to four times a week.

Bathing Habits

Budgies are not fond of bathing and it may be difficult to induce your bird to bathe. Toys in a birdbath sometimes help, or try putting your bird's favorite greens in the water; these will often lure a bird into its bath. If neither of these bribes work, spray your bird lightly with water from an atomizer bottle or hold your pet under a gently spraying faucet.

Breeding Budgies

Budgies will breed during all seasons of the year. They breed easily and are fun to raise. The mating pair of birds should be about one year old and should meet each other while still in their own cages. After two or three days you can transfer them both to a cage that is large enough to hold a nesting box.

While birds are mating and raising their young, it is a good idea to soak their seed mixture in water before feeding it to them. Also, add one teaspoonful of cod-liver oil to each pint of seed. Be certain that the oil is mixed thoroughly with the seed. The oil will help prevent egg binding in your hen.

NESTING BOX—Your nesting box, sometimes called a breeding box, should be six inches square and nine to ten inches high and should be attached to the cage. The bottom of the box should be concave to keep the eggs from rolling about and breaking; there should be an entrance hole two inches square.

Your budgie does not need to prepare her nest; she will lay her eggs on bare wood. Once she is ready, it takes her at least a week to lay the first egg; she will then lay four to six eggs on

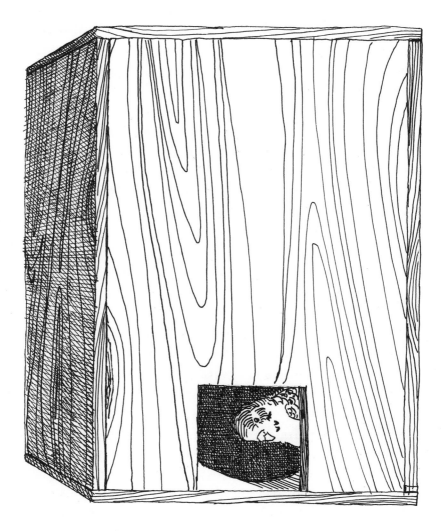

A budgerigar nesting box

alternate days. Be careful not to disturb the cage; cleaning the cage at this time is less important than allowing your pet to remain quiet. The eggs will take approximately eighteen days to hatch. Baby budgies will then be born every other day for a week to ten days.

During the period of incubation, the hen sits on her eggs to keep them warm and safe. It is interesting to watch the male feed her. He gives her partially digested, regurgitated food, commonly called "pigeon milk." Baby budgies are also fed pigeon milk. When the babies are about four weeks old, they will leave their nest and begin to feed themselves. At this time remove the young birds to their own cage.

Do not overbreed your birds. Budgies should not be allowed to hatch more than four clutches a year. Many diseases result from overbreeding.

Your budgie can be a wonderful pet; keep it healthy and happy.

PARRAKEETS

A budgerigar is only one member of a vast family of parrakeets. Most of the other members of this family are more expensive than the budgie and some species are extremely rare. Although all parrakeets have small bills, long tails, and slight bodies, their size differs considerably from genus to genus. All members of the parrakeet family are, however, basically cared for in the same way. To assure proper care for your bird, more detailed information should be researched. (See "For Further Reading," at the end of the book.)

COCKATIELS

The Cockatiel ranks second only to the budgie as the most popular pet bird in America. Native to Australia and the island of Tasmania, this member of the parrot family has been bred in Holland for hundreds of years; breeders in England began raising Cockatiels around 1850 and from there they came to the United States.

The Cockatiel, known by the Australians as the Quarrion, is the tamest, best-natured, and gentlest bird of the parrot family. It is a clean bird, and many bird fanciers claim that it is the cleanest cage bird available. It is extremely hardy and, when well cared for, usually has a life span from ten to fourteen years.

A Cockatiel will live happily alongside budgies or other small parrot-family birds. It is easily trained and can learn to whistle, talk, and even perform tricks. A male cockie will learn to talk more readily than a female one, but with patience a female can also be taught to speak fairly well.

Description
of a Cockatiel

The Cockatiel is a long, slender bird; the male appears to have a slimmer body than the female and also a longer neck. The average Cockatiel ranges from eleven to fourteen inches in length, although in their natural habitat they often grow longer. Their wingspan can spread up to sixteen inches in width. The color of both the male and the female ranges from a dusky to a dark gray, and both sexes have a prominent white band stretching along the side of each wing. Both male and female cockies have graceful lemon-yellow crests tipped with brown feathers. The forepart of the head and the sides of the face and the throat are lemon-yellow in the male; the sides of his crown are white. The female's coloring is much the same, but lacks the lemon and white areas present on the head of the male. Both male and female birds have bright orange, circular splashes of color on their cheeks, and the underside of their long, graceful tails is dark slate gray. The adult female has dark bar markings on her tail.

Baby cockies look much like adult females, and it is extremely difficult to determine their sex before the age of six

months. Between six months and a year, the sex of the young male becomes apparent by the yellow color on his head and face.

Type of Cage

Because of the large wingspan of the Cockatiel, it is essential that you house your bird in a fairly large cage. A parrot's cage is ideal in that it is large enough to permit your bird to exercise.

Your cage should be equipped with several perches placed far enough from the side of the cage so that your bird doesn't hit its tail when sitting or swinging. Though a Cockatiel is a small bird, its feet are comparatively large. Perches, therefore, should be changed when they appear to be worn down from repeated scrapings. It is also advisable to have perches of varying sizes. These will help prevent possible deformities from developing in a young Cockatiel's feet.

Cockatiels, like most parrot-related birds, love to chew on things; they are fond of furniture and particularly like to tear paper. This desire can be satisfied by placing some branches in the cage. Be certain you choose nonpoisonous trees such as fruit trees, willow trees, and maple trees.

Toys

Cockies are fond of toys and will play with a bell or swing on a musical perch for hours. If your bird is a female, buy a plastic baby bird. Your little cockie will treat it like one of

*Cockatiels are
both loving and
trainable birds.*

her own; she will mother it for hours. If you have a male bird, try putting a mirror in the cage. Males love to preen before a mirror as well as whistle and jabber to their own image.

Food

A Cockatiel is not a choosy eater and will, in fact, eat almost anything; unselective eating can be fatal. A Cockatiel should be fed a mixture of Parrakeet Seed, oats, and sunflower seed daily. Mix three-fourths of a teaspoon of cod-liver oil and a few drops of wheat germ into each quart of seed mixture. In addition, once or twice a week, your little pet can indulge in some greens; for a change you might try the wedge of an apple. Spray millet is always received as a special treat.

Milksop is particularly important for Cockatiels and should, if possible, be given to your cockie daily. It is made by soaking whole wheat bread in milk and then wringing the bread dry. It *must* be changed daily, as the milk sours readily and can make your bird ill.

Your cockie should have a cuttlebone or crushed oyster shell in his cage.

Water

Water cups should be changed and cleaned daily. Cockies often enjoy playing with the water in their cups. At times you may find that the water has become so dirty that it must be changed twice in one day.

Bathing Habits

If your Cockatiel is to maintain a healthy appearance, bathing is a must. Once cockies become accustomed to water, they usually grow to love their baths. Patience, therefore, is of utmost importance when first introducing your pet to a bath—if you frighten your bird at the start, you may have trouble in the future.

Never spray your Cockatiel with commercial bird sprays that are recommended to prevent mites and bring sheen to feathers. These sprays are fine for all other birds, but Cockatiels have a powdery slough on their feathers which should not be sprayed with any substance that has an oil base. Plain water is the best and only liquid to use on your Cockatiel.

Breeding

Cockatiels are extremely easy to breed and a hen will often lay as many as eight eggs in a clutch.

The nesting box for a cockie is similar to that of a budgie. An ideal size is ten inches square by fourteen inches deep; the hole to enter the box should be at least three inches high. The box should have a perch which is five-eighths to three-quarters inch in diameter.

As a rule both male and female take turns sitting on the eggs; curiously, the male seems to keep them warm during the day while the female broods at night. The eggs incubate in approximately eighteen to twenty days. It is important not to disturb the nest until the baby cockies have ventured out on their own. Adult Cockatiels may refuse to feed babies that have been touched by humans.

Cockatiels should be at least one year old before being bred. It is advisable to have only a single pair of cockies in a cage when they are breeding. During the breeding period it is absolutely essential that cockies be given a large flight area in which to exercise if they are to give birth to healthy offspring.

PARROTS

For thousands of years the talking parrot has been a favorite pet. Until the eighteenth century only the wealthy could afford to own a parrot, as both the bird and its ornate cage were extremely costly. By the nineteenth century, bird fanciers of every economic class began keeping parrots as pets and housing them in simple cages. Until recently, many species of parrots were available and could be purchased at a nominal cost. Since 1972, however, when the United States government forbade the importation of all foreign birds into the country, the price of parrots has so skyrocketed that a parrot can no longer be considered a popular pet. The two best-known parrot species, the Amazon and the African gray, now range in price between $250 and $1000.

It is interesting that, although parrots can be found in a myriad of shapes and sizes, they all have certain general characteristics: large heads in proportion to their body size; hooked bills which are extremely strong; mallet-shaped tongues; and sturdy feet. They have long, broad tails which are usually one-fourth the total length of their bodies, and they are primarily vegetarians. All parrot-family birds seem to have a remarkable ability to mimic human sounds, although some species learn to speak far more readily than others.

AFRICAN LOVEBIRDS

African Lovebirds are shaped exactly like miniature parrots. As their name suggests, their native habitat is Africa. They

*African Lovebirds
make intelligent pets.*

are bright, colorful birds ranging from four inches to five and a half inches in length. They have large heads and stocky bodies and, like the parrot, they have hard, curved beaks.

Lovebirds make excellent pets. They are hardy, long-lived, and breed easily. They are, however, usually aggressive with other birds and should, therefore, be kept to themselves. They are not always easy to tame, but once you have succeeded in taming your bird, you will find it is extremely intelligent, quick to learn tricks, and easily taught to talk.

Type of Cage

Lovebirds will live happily in a standard-size budgie cage, equipped in a similar manner to that of a budgie's.

Food and bathing habits also closely parallel that of budgie birds. Their feed consists of a mixture of Parrakeet Seed, sunflower seed, whole hulled oats, and large millet seed. Health grit, a cuttlebone, and a supply of oyster shell are a must. Greens and fruit should also be added three or four times a week. (See section on "Feeding Your Budgie," page 23.)

Breeding

Lovebirds breed freely. They nest happily in a standard-size budgie nesting box. Unlike budgies, however, Lovebirds build elaborate nests. They should be provided with a variety of nesting materials such as palm leaves, bamboo leaves, green bark strips from trees, grasses, hay, and even feathers. Other nesting materials include four- to six-inch lengths of raffia and six-inch squares of burlap which your birds will strip into strands on their own. The nesting material should not be dried. Green leaves provide moisture which is necessary to keep the shells of the eggs soft so that the baby chicks are able to peck their way out at hatching time.

Breeding seasons vary. Some Lovebirds prefer to breed in the fall, while others prefer the spring. Lovebirds will mate readily; however, sexing Lovebirds is extremely difficult, and in the species available in the United States, almost impossible. It is quite common for two hens to act as a pair. They will even lay eggs, but their eggs will, of course, never hatch.

If you are lucky enough to have a male and female bird, breeding them will not be a problem. Like budgies, they lay their eggs every other day and usually lay seven or eight eggs in a clutch. Eggs hatch in approximately twenty-one days. It takes baby Lovebirds about five weeks to leave their nest during the day, and another two weeks or so before they feel secure enough to be away from the nest at night.

MYNAH BIRDS

Mynah birds are found chiefly in the jungle highlands of India and Thailand. They are rarely bred in captivity, probably because it is impossible to differentiate between the sexes. Government restrictions on importing foreign birds have made the price of Mynahs, like parrots, prohibitive; it is virtually impossible to buy a baby Mynah.

If you are lucky enough to obtain a Mynah, however, you will have a wonderful pet. These sleek black birds are better talkers than parrots and can even mimic intonations in a human voice when repeating words.

Unlike the birds of the parrot family, the Mynah is a soft-billed bird and cannot crack seeds. Its natural diet, therefore, consists of insects, fruits, and berries. Commercially prepared food for Mynahs is available and will provide your bird with its nutritional needs. This food can be supplemented with any fruit cut into small pieces, as well as such diverse foods

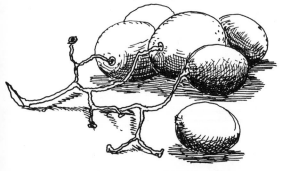

as raw ground meat, hard-boiled egg, baked sweet potato, whole wheat bread, and greens. Healthy Mynahs seem to eat all day long and should have a supply of food in their cage at all times. Because Mynahs do not eat seed, they do not require either grit or gravel.

Mynahs are even better talkers than parrots.

Finches

Finches make up one-half of the birds of the world and one species or another can be found wherever you travel. Finches are small birds and exist in every possible color. The most popular finches kept as pets in this country are the Australian Finch and the Java Temple Bird. Canaries, also of the finch family, will be discussed separately.

The Zebra Finch and the Lady Gould, both species of the Australian Finch family, are inexpensive and easy to raise. Neither of these birds is easily trained, but they are delightful to watch and to listen to and can be very happy even though confined to cage life.

The Zebra Finch is found in a variety of colors, but all zebras have a black-and-white-barred chest with an orange beak and orange legs. The Lady Gould looks as though bright splotches of color were painted on its feathers. Lady Goulds are not only beautiful, but they also have a lovely, sweet song.

The Java Temple Bird has a black head, a gray body, and a black tail. Its white face is highlighted with rings of red around the eyes and a pink bill. It can be tamed more easily than the Zebra or the Lady Gould, and with a little patience it can even be finger-trained. These birds are also known as Java Rice Birds; in the Orient they are considered pests, as they often devour large crops of rice.

The bird at the top of the cage is a Zebra Finch; the pair are Java Temple Birds.

Type of Cage

Finches can live happily in a fairly small cage, but be certain that the bars of the cage are not more than five-eighths of an inch apart. A finch can easily slip through bars that are more widely spaced.

Finches, like all birds, need to exercise. Flight cages for finches are relatively small, the average one being twenty-one inches deep, twenty-six inches high, and thirty inches wide; even apartment dwellers, therefore, should provide a finch with space to fly about.

Feeding Your Finch

Finches are seed eaters and will thrive on commercial finch food. They should be given greens two to three times a week and occasional treats of wedges of unpeeled apples and oranges. A millet spray should be placed inside the cage. On very special days, treat your little pet to a few mealworms or any insects you can find in the backyard.

HEALTH GRIT should be placed in the cage daily.

WATER. Change daily.

CUTTLEBONE. One cuttlebone should be attached to the cage for each finch. A fresh cuttlebone should be given to each finch monthly.

Bathing Habits

Finches usually enjoy taking a bath and should be allowed to do so daily.

Breeding

The most important step in the successful mating of finches is to prepare them in advance. Birds must be in breeding condition before they are mated and before the hen is allowed to make her nest. In order to prepare your finches for mating, it is important to feed them special nesting food.

NESTING FOOD RECIPE. Prepare a mixture of five to six tablespoons English Nestling food or cooked farina, two tablespoons Royal Lunch crackers rolled into crumbs, two hard-boiled eggs (not only mashed but put through a sieve), one to two tablespoons strained carrots (baby food is ideal).

This mixture should be kept under refrigeration and each batch of the recipe not used after the second day, as the hard-boiled egg tends to spoil.

Begin feeding the nesting food to your finch in February, as finches breed once a year, sometime between the middle of March and the end of June. Accustom your bird to this mixture by feeding it to her once a week; gradually increase the number of feedings until your hen is eating it daily. The mixture can also be fed to a male finch without ill effect.

Next, buy some nesting material from your pet dealer. Place it inside the cage near a closed nest box; a cardboard shoe box is fine. Zebra Finches prefer a basket nest, but will accept a box. If your birds are not attracted to the nesting material, change its position in the cage. Sooner or later your finches will decide to build a nest.

Once your hen has laid her first egg, discontinue the nesting food. After the eggs have hatched, you may reintroduce the nesting formula once a week, as finches will happily nest twice in one season.

Zebra Finches are probably the easiest of the finches to breed. Lady Goulds can prove difficult, for the hens do not take care of their young and are often unconcerned about their eggs during the incubation period—approximately twelve days. When conditioning Lady Goulds, therefore, you should condition at least one pair of Zebras at the same time. As soon as your Lady Gould hen lays her eggs, they should be removed from the nest and given to the Zebra hen to hatch. Be careful; finch eggs are extremely fragile.

NOTE: Since Zebra Finches mature a few days earlier than Lady Goulds, it is important to watch that the Zebra does not desert her foster chicks before they are old enough to feed themselves. If this occurs, it probably indicates that the hen is ready to make a second nest. Remove her to another cage; the male Zebra will take over the responsibility of feeding the chicks.

The Java Temple Bird is easy to raise but it is extremely difficult to sex these birds; this, of course, makes the success of breeding uncertain. If you do have a pair, however, they will build an elaborate nest in any small nesting box, provided that they have the necessary material on hand.

Unlike the Zebra and the Lady Gould finches, Java Temple Birds do not require nesting food. Their eggs incubate in approximately thirteen days and there are usually three to six eggs in a clutch. The nest should not be touched until the baby birds are weaned. This usually takes five to six weeks. Once the young can feed themselves, they should be placed in a separate cage.

Canaries

The beautiful little canary has been a favorite of bird lovers since Roman times. As early as the first century A.D., Pliny, the Roman historian, wrote of this lovely songbird which had been found in great numbers in the Canary Islands off the west coast of Africa. It is interesting to note that although the Canary bird was named for its native homeland, this seven-island group was named Canarias after the large canines (dogs) found there by the Romans.

The sweet song of the canary made it a sought-after pet in Europe from at least the early sixteenth century; after 1622 it became one of the most popular household pets. In that year a ship carrying a load of wild canaries was wrecked in the Mediterranean. The little birds, aided by the winds, flew all over Europe and were adopted by bird lovers everywhere they went.

Description of Canaries

The canary is a member of the finch family and, like all finches, is a seed eater. Canaries, today, barely resemble the wild green birds that were first captured. Years of selected breeding have produced a bright yellow male bird; the female canary is not as attractive and is a greenish-yellow color. Both sexes are about four inches long. Canary breeders have also produced canaries in a variety of colors, including a lizard canary with variegated markings resembling a lizard.

There are two types of song canaries—the "chopper" canary and the "roller" canary. The chopper is the most popular song canary. If you listen to it carefully you will hear the words: "chop, chop, chop," in place of the lyrics of a song. The chopper is a hardy little bird, a beautiful singer, and easy to care for.

Roller canaries are also beautiful singers, but their song is softer and more mellow than that of the chopper's. If you are considering entering your canary in a song contest, a good roller's song is far superior to that of an equally good chopper's.

A canary has an average life span of approximately eight years. You can determine the age of a canary by looking at its legs; a scaly leg condition is a sign of age.

Beware of advertisements stating: "Unsexed canaries for sale." Females are neither as pretty nor as good singers as males. You can be almost 100 percent certain that in buying an unsexed bird you are buying a female one. Remember the old cliché: "You get what you pay for." CAUTION: Don't buy a canary during molting season—July to October. Moving a bird while it is molting or about to molt will not only upset it, but can result in death.

Type
of Cage

Buy a simple canary cage, the larger the better.

Equip your cage with feed dishes, water dish, dish for health grit, and a cuttlebone. You can add one extra cup for treat seed.

PERCHES. Unlike perches for parrot family birds, perches in a canary's cage can be washed instead of scraped; canaries are not generally troubled with rheumatism.

Choppers and
rollers are both
beautiful singers.

Food

Feed your canary standard prepared canary seed. Three to four times a week feed your bird greens or sprouting birdseed. Do not leave greens in your cage more than one-half to one hour.

Bathing Habits

Most canaries prefer to bathe in a small dish placed on the floor of the cage. If your canary decides not to bathe, spray it lightly with water. Never force your bird into a bath.

Breeding

Canaries are easy and fun to breed. Like all finches, they breed in the spring. This means that you should buy your pair of birds not later than December so that they have time to adjust to their new surroundings. Begin feeding your birds nesting food about one month before you are ready to breed them. (See recipe on page 41 for finches.) In addition, conditioning seed should be supplied daily.

If you do not want to make nesting food, there are several commercial soft foods on the market for this purpose.

Do not keep mixture more than two days. Any spilled or uneaten nesting food should be removed from the cage, as the mixture will sour and become poisonous.

Before you attempt to breed your canaries, separate the male and the female birds; place them in a double breeding cage with a solid, but removable, centerpiece. A good-size breeding cage is twenty-four inches by eighteen inches by twelve inches. Keep the birds apart for several days. When the male is ready to mate, he will become restless and begin singing loudly. When the hen is ready she, too, will begin singing, and, in addition, her vents will become enlarged. At this time, remove the solid center and replace it with a wire partition. (Every breeding cage comes equipped with both a glass and a

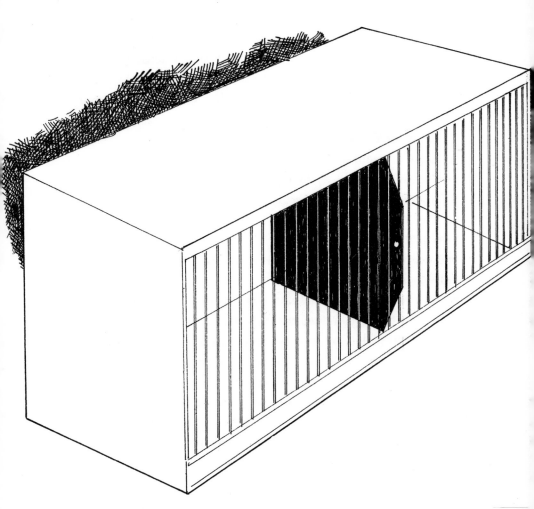

*A double breeding
cage for canaries*

wire partition.) As soon as the male begins to feed the hen
through the wires, you can feel relatively certain that the birds
are ready to mate; now remove the partition. If the pair begin
to fight, they are not quite ready and should be separated for
another five to seven days.

Once your pair of canaries seems happy together, place a metal, felt-lined nesting pan inside the cage. A kitchen strainer is particularly well suited for a nesting pan. Remove the handle and fasten the strainer about halfway up the side of the cage. Then, gradually give your hen nesting material such as short pieces of soft string or cotton, dried grass, and moss. Nesting supplies are sold at all pet shops that handle birds. Take care not to give your birds long strands of any material, as both baby and adult birds can become entangled in them.

After the hen has completed her nest, she will take approximately eight days to lay her first egg. Then she will lay one egg a day for the next few days. The normal clutch contains three to five eggs. Each time your canary lays an egg, remove it from the clutch, and replace it with a dummy egg you can buy in your pet store. Place the real egg in a lined box and keep the box in a fairly cool place. Repeat this until your hen has finished laying her eggs. Then, remove the dummy eggs and replace the original eggs. The hen will now begin the hatching process which will take about fourteen days. If you follow the above procedure, the eggs will hatch together, and the chicks will all be well attended by the mother.

Continue feeding your canaries soft food, conditioning seed, and green foods.

If the female decides to nest again before her fledglings are self-feeding, separate babies and male from female by means of the wire partition. The male canary will take care of the offspring.

As soon as the babies are self-feeding they can be weaned from the parents and removed to a separate cage. Continue feeding the babies with soft food until they finish their first molt—about twelve weeks old. Then decrease the amounts of soft food gradually until the birds are eating seed with no difficulties.

Pigeons and Doves

Pigeons and their smaller cousins, doves, are among the oldest domesticated birds. At least as early as 3000 B.C., Egyptians raised pigeons for food. Centuries later the pigeon began to be developed as a show bird and a pet. There are many kinds of pigeons, ranging from common gray birds to exotic birds with interesting and diversified colorings. They are found the world over, but most of them are not considered household pets. Nevertheless, pigeons can be great fun if you are able to provide adequate outdoor caging. As with all birds, a young pigeon, or a squab, is easier to tame than an adult bird.

Food

Pigeons will thrive on a good pigeon mix, readily available at any pet store. You can prepare your own feed by mixing whole corn (not cracked corn), wheat, dried peas, rye kafir, barley, and hulled oats.

Health is essential for the digestive system of pigeons. Ground oyster shells are an important part of the diet. Pigeons need salt, and this is most easily fed to them in the form of a salt lick. Occasional greens add variety to your pet's diet. Pigeons should be fed twice daily.

Feeding your pigeon is the fastest way of taming the stocky bird.

Give your pet fresh drinking water daily. In addition, supply your bird with a large shallow bowl, half filled with water, for bathing. If your pigeon does not naturally enjoy bathing, induce it to bathe daily by placing a few greens in the bath water.

Breeding

Pigeons are one of the easiest birds to breed successfully. All you need to do is provide your pair with nesting material such as coarse straw or hay cut into five-inch strips. If you wish, you can give your pigeons a nest box, but this is not necessary.

Both male and female share in building the nest and both birds take turns incubating the eggs. The hen usually broods from dusk to dawn; the male broods during the day. The hen usually has two eggs in her clutch. She lays them approximately a day and a half apart. The eggs hatch in about eighteen days. Both parents share in feeding the young squabs with pigeon milk. The squabs can be weaned and left on their own within five weeks.

DOVES

The peaceful dove is perhaps the most intelligent member of the pigeon family and certainly the most graceful. First mentioned in the Biblical story of Noah, the dove has remained a symbol of peace for more than five thousand years.

Doves are particularly gentle birds and make wonderful pets. They are hardy birds, easily tamed, and can be housed in a fairly small cage.

Food

Smaller than their pigeon cousins, doves cannot eat a coarse pigeon feed. They will, however, thrive on prepared budgie or finch food, and they can also be fed a wild-bird mix. Green food should be added to their diet three to four times a week.

The top bird is a pigeon,
the bottom a
ring-necked turtle dove.

Like all seed-eating birds, doves need health grit to help digest their food. Budgie-size grit is recommended.

Bathing Habits

Doves usually like bathing and, like pigeons, should be provided with a large shallow bowl and be allowed to bathe at least three times a week.

Breeding

Doves breed easily in exactly the same manner as their larger cousins. (See "Breeding," page 51.)

Illness and Broken Bones

Birds, like humans, are susceptible to diseases, have accidents, and break bones. Unlike humans, however, sick birds do not recover readily. Taking good care of your bird, therefore, is the best medicine. A bird that is well fed, has fresh water daily, and is not in drafts or direct sunlight will usually stay well. Furthermore, your pet needs exercise in order to stay fit. Broken bones are often the result of someone or something frightening your bird, causing it to flap around frantically. In the event that your bird should become sick or is injured, be certain to have the name of a veterinarian who cares for birds.

General Care of a Sick Bird

An ailing bird should always be isolated from other birds and kept warm. Put a 25-watt light bulb over the cage or a heating pad—with a cover to prevent soiling—under it to help maintain a temperature of about 90° F. Cover three sides of the cage with an insulating cloth, preferably in a light color, to maintain the heat. Be careful that the light bulb does not burn the cloth. These measures are of utmost importance. Once a bird gets cold, it becomes listless and usually stops eating. If your bird does not appear to be better in two to three days, get in touch with your veterinarian. A bird that stops eating rarely lives more than a few days. Remove toys and perches from a sick bird's cage and try to keep it as quiet as possible.

The following is a list of the most common ailments of birds:

COLDS. They are usually caused by drafts. Symptoms are similar to those of a human: runny nose, sneezing, difficulty in breathing, lack of appetite, and watery eyes.

Keeping a sick bird warm

Treatment: Isolate the bird immediately; colds are contagious. Your pet dealer should carry nose drops and inhalants. Antibiotics such as aureomycin may be helpful. Follow rules for "General Care of a Sick Bird." A cold that is unattended can develop into pneumonia. Treatment is the same as for a cold, but antibiotics are imperative.

CONSTIPATION. Infrequent, hard, whitish droppings are a sign of constipation. This ailment can usually be cleared up by adding more greens to your bird's diet. Watercress is particularly helpful. If this remedy is not successful, consult your veterinarian.

DIARRHEA. Loose droppings are usually caused by eating too many greens. Commercial remedies are available. A weak tea solution, instead of plain water, is sometimes helpful. Another useful remedy is a mixture of one tablespoon of black-strap molasses added to a pint of boiled water. This is a nourishing supplement and will usually clear up the problem within three to four days. If diarrhea persists or is bloody, consult your veterinarian at once.

EYE INFLAMMATION. Often the result of a cold. Cleanse eyes four times a day with a mild solution of boric acid and warm water. Dry thoroughly.

EGG BINDING. Occasionally a hen will be unable to pass an egg that she is attempting to lay. This is an extremely pain-

Helping an egg-bound hen

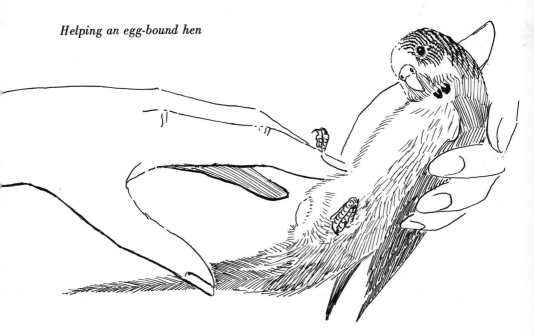

ful occurrence, and if the egg is not released, the hen will die. Gently remove the hen from her nest and place her in a lined box warmed from below with an electric heating pad or light bulb. Be careful not to let the temperature exceed 80° F.; after an hour, if the egg is still bound within the hen, raise the temperature to 95° F. maximum. Sometimes a few drops of cod-liver oil or mineral oil, dropped into the vent with an eyedropper, will lubricate the opening and make the passing of the egg much easier. As a last resort, apply gentle pressure to the abdomen just above the egg. Be extremely careful that you press lightly enough so that the egg does not break. Once the egg has passed, the hen will rapidly return to normal. It is not advisable to breed this hen until the next season. Proper diet and exercise usually avoid the problem of egg binding.

MOLTING. This is a healthy, normal occurrence. Once a year all birds shed their feathers and shiny new ones grow in their stead. During the six-week molting period, a bird's resistance is lowered and it is more susceptible to colds. A small amount of molting food should be added to the regular food. Discontinue molting food as soon as the molting process is completed. In addition to an annual molt, some birds undergo a partial molt in the course of the year. This, too, is normal.

FRENCH MOLT. This premature and continual molting of feathers will drain a bird of all its vitality. There are many opinions as to the cause and cure of this ailment, but no one has really discovered the answer to either. The disease usually affects budgies, but it has been known to attack Cockatiels and Lovebirds. Some aviarists believe that molting is caused by tiny mites which attack the feathers of these birds; others believe the cause is temperature change. The following remedies may prove helpful: Remove your bird to a cooler location; spray bird and cage at frequent intervals to kill any mites present; add a few drops of wheat germ oil to your bird's diet.

MITES. There are many types of mites that are harmful to birds, but red mites are the most destructive. These tiny creatures only attack birds at night. As a rule the pinpoint-sized mites attack small birds such as budgies, finches, and canaries. The mites are red because they are bloodsuckers. A swarm of mites can drain enough blood from a small bird to cause death. In order to see if mites are present, cover your cage at night with a white flannel cloth—the red bodies will show up clearly against the white background. To get rid of mites, remove the bird from the cage and scald the cage thoroughly; spray the cage with any mild insecticide that does not contain DDT. Do not try to take the mites off the bird. If spraying the cage does not work, see your vet.

FITS AND APOPLEXY. Occasionally a bird will be found at the bottom of its cage with its head thrown back, flapping its wings wildly against the floor. A fit of this nature is usually caused by poor diet or a sudden change of diet. Vitamin supplements added to the feed will usually clear up the ailment. A bird having a fit should be placed in a warm, dark corner and left alone until the fit passes.

Apoplexy is a frequent cause of death. There is no cure for this disease, which is usually the result of a ruptured blood vessel in the brain or heart. Apoplexy is frequently the result of overexcitement, excessive heat, or a poor diet.

SORE FEET. A bird with a clean cage and clean perches, which are not overly worn down, will rarely have sore feet. Soothing commercial ointments to treat sore feet are available at most pet stores.

SCALES. Inflamed scales on a bird's legs appear as a white, crusty covering; they are usually caused by mites. Mite-killing salve should be applied to the affected area. This will smother mites and soften scales.

REGURGITATION. Birds will vomit up a sour crop, but most

birds regurgitate because of their desire to mate. They feed their young the partially digested, regurgitated food known as pigeon milk.

PARROT FEVER OR ORNITHOSIS. Although it is named parrot fever, all birds are susceptible to this virus. This disease, which can be transmitted to humans, is no longer feared, for antibiotics have been found that are effective against the deadly ornithosis virus. True parrot fever is difficult to diagnose, and an accurate diagnosis can be confirmed only with a blood test. The incidence of parrot fever is exceedingly rare.

BROKEN BONES. Simple fractures are usually best left alone. They will heal in seven to ten days. Assist your pet by placing food and water on the floor. Badly torn or compound fractures should be put in a splint; it is advisable to consult your veterinarian.

REMEMBER—Most accidents and most ailments can be avoided. Proper diet, exercise, cleanliness, and care are the best medicine to maintain a healthy, happy bird.

Avoid broken bones—
keep other pets
away from your bird.

Glossary

Aviary. A large enclosure for keeping birds.

Aviculture. The breeding of and caring for birds.

Aviculturist. One who is concerned with maintaining conditions to improve the health and longevity of birds.

Brood. A hen sitting on her eggs during incubation period.

Cere. Waxy piece of skin that grows above a bird's beak.

Clutch. The number of eggs produced by a hen at one time.

Fledgling. A young bird.

Ornithology. The study of birds.

Pigeon milk. Partially digested food that is regurgitated into the mouth of the young.

Primaries. The outside flight feathers of a bird, situated nearest to the abdomen.

Quill. The hollow stem of the feather.

Slough. A powdery substance like dandruff on a Cockatiel's feathers.

To sex. To determine whether a bird is a male or a female.

For Further Reading

Ames, Felicia. *The Bird You Care For*. New York: Signet Book, 1970.

Bates, Henry J., and Busenbark, Robert. *Parrots and Related Birds*. Neptune City, N.J.: T.F.H. Publications, Inc., 1969.

Stroud, Robert. *Stroud's Digest on the Diseases of Birds*. Neptune City, N.J.: T.F.H. Publications, Inc.

Villiard, Paul. *Birds as Pets*. Garden City, N.Y.: Doubleday & Company, Inc., 1974.

Index

About the Author

Joan Joseph is a graduate of McGill University and has studied at the University of Southern California, the Université d'Aix-Marseille, and the University of Paris. She holds a foundation grant for historical research on thirteenth-century England and has spent a good deal of time in London on this project. She has owned a number of different species of pet birds and has bred some of them. Joan Joseph is the author of many books for young people.